Who Was Poor Richard?
Colonials to Remember

by Carl W. Grody

HOUGHTON MIFFLIN　　　　BOSTON

Benjamin Franklin's kite experiment, June, 1752

Benjamin Franklin: Common and Uncommon

We think of Benjamin Franklin as a scientist with a great imagination. He was the man who proved the link between lightning and electricity by flying his kite in a thunderstorm. But Franklin was also gifted with a great mind for common sense. And he had the ability to persuade people to follow his advice.

Franklin saw himself as a common man. He hobnobbed with the rich and famous. But he also had a strong connection with the average person on the street.

That showed in his *Poor Richard's Almanack*. He published it once a year. The book contained weather and farm reports. But Franklin filled in empty space with common sense sayings, such as "A penny saved is a penny earned" and "Early to bed, early to rise, makes a man healthy, wealthy, and wise."

Writing his almanac was just one of the ways Franklin used his inquiring mind. He was also an inventor and a craftsman. He invented the lightning rod. He invented the Franklin stove. He invented swim fins and the rocking chair and bifocals. But he never patented his inventions. He said they were for the common good, to be of the greatest help to the most people.

Franklin always thought about the common good. He started the first fire department. He started the first library. He started the postal system. He created a college and a hospital.

Franklin also made a fortune as a printer. But it was his work for the public that made him happy. He did not like to talk in public. He worked behind the scenes. He became friends with powerful people. He then changed their minds with long letters and even longer discussions.

Franklin was an Englishman at heart. He first thought that the American colonies should stay part of the British Empire. He worked for years to keep the British and Americans together. He even spent seventeen years in Britain as a representative of the colonies. He told the British they would gain more by treating the colonies as equal members of the empire. But the British insisted on treating the colonies as their subjects.

Both countries argued about who was in charge in America. The British said the colonies belonged to them. The Americans said they should govern themselves. The British taxed the colonies to help cover the cost of an expensive war with France in North America. The colonists wanted to break away from the British.

There was a limit to even Franklin's patience. He had warned the British for years that war was coming with America. He pleaded with the British to stop taxing the colonies.

But Franklin finally gave up. He returned to America. He helped write the Declaration of Independence. Then Franklin sailed for France to ask for help in the war against the British.

Franklin stayed in France for the entire Revolutionary War. He talked the French into giving the Americans guns and money. His ability to talk the French into helping probably won the war for America.

Franklin was one of three Americans to negotiate with the British for their surrender in 1781. He stayed in France a few more years before returning to Philadelphia in 1785.

Franklin thought he was done with public service. But he was wrong. He was the oldest delegate to work on the constitution at the Constitutional Convention in 1787. He was so old that he couldn't walk in and out of the building. Four convicts carried him in a sedan chair.

Franklin argued against slavery. He became the president of an anti-slavery group. He also wrote a major paper that said slavery should be outlawed.

Franklin wrote one of his last letters to a friend in England. He wrote, "God grant that not only the love of liberty, but a thorough knowledge of the rights of man, may pervade all the nations of the earth, and say, 'This is my country . . .'"

Benjamin Franklin

Franklin died April 17, 1790. Twenty thousand people came to his funeral. He was buried under a surprisingly simple gravestone. His last will and testament was just as simple. It started, "I, Benjamin Franklin, printer . . ."

That was why people trusted Franklin. He was one of the most important men in history. But he saw himself as no better than the common person.

Olaudah Equiano: Voice of the Enslaved

Franklin spoke for the common person. Olaudah Equiano spoke for enslaved people. His voice is one of the few that have come down to us through history telling about the experience of slavery during colonial times.

Equiano was an African who came to America in chains. He eventually was able to buy his freedom. But he never forgot what it was like to be enslaved. He even wrote a first-person account about it in 1789. His book was the first to be written from the point of view of an enslaved person.

Equiano was born in Benin, which is now part of Nigeria in Africa. Many of the men in his family worked as judges. Equiano was supposed to be one, too. His father even took him to court so he could see the way things worked.

But Benin was not a safe place. Benin's leaders sold their own people into slavery as early as the 1400s. Nobody truly felt safe there. People were kidnapped and sold into slavery on a regular basis.

It happened to Equiano and his sister when he was eleven years old. They stayed together for a few days. Then they were separated. Equiano passed from master to master until he reached the coastline six months later.

There he saw a white man for the first time — a lot of white men, in fact. They threw him onto a slave ship headed for the West Indies. They forced him into the slave hold with other captured Africans. Equiano lived there for the long trip across the Atlantic Ocean. This was called the middle passage.

Olaudah Equiano

Equiano later wrote about the trip in his autobiography. He described "the shrieks of the women." He wrote about "the groans of the dying." It was so bad that some of the Africans wanted to commit suicide. Some managed to drown themselves. They were envied by the others.

But Equiano was lucky compared to the other enslaved Africans. Nobody bought him when the ship reached the West

7

Indies. So he was shipped to Virginia. There a lieutenant in the British Royal Navy bought him. They moved back to England, where Equiano educated himself. Then they traveled around the world in the lieutenant's ships. Equiano became a good navigator.

Equiano bought his freedom in 1766. He might not have been able to do that if he had been working on a plantation in the American colonies. Americans demanded freedom from Britain. They fought for rights due to "any man." But they would not give the same rights to their enslaved Africans.

The situation was different in England. Many British thought slavery was wrong. The British courts backed them up. In 1765, a judge declared that any enslaved African became a free man when he set foot on British soil.

Another judge went even further in 1772. Lord Mansfield, the Lord Chief Justice of the King's Bench, said an owner could not force his enslaved African back to the West Indies from England. That meant that a slave would be free if he reached England.

But many British ships still traded slaves outside its borders. Critics wanted to make all slave trade illegal, whether or not it was in England. Many people wrote and argued against slavery. But nobody had the impact of Equiano.

Equiano wrote a book about slavery. It showed how badly the enslaved were treated, especially on slave ships. Equiano spoke directly to Britain's Parliament as he wrote. He wanted to convince it to outlaw slavery altogether. He did convince many members of Parliament.

But Parliament refused to outlaw slavery then because of what was happening across the English Channel in France. The French Revolution made the British nervous about any great social change. The idea of outlawing slavery was pushed aside for a few years.

Finally, in 1807, the British passed the Bill for the Abolition of the Slave Trade. Equiano had died ten years before that, but his legacy lived on in that bill.

Mary Musgrove: Mediator between Two Nations

Mary Musgrove was born in 1700. Her birth name was Coosaponakeesa. She was half Creek (Yamacraw) Indian and half British. Her mother was a niece of the leader of the Creek nation. Her father was a British trader from the South Carolina colony.

Mary lived with the Creeks until she was ten years old. Then she went to live in South Carolina with her father's people. She learned to deal with both whites and American Indians. That made her the perfect person to help create the colony of Georgia.

The idea for the colony of Georgia came from General James Oglethorpe. He was a British military officer with a big heart. He especially worried about the people in debtor's prison. That was where people went when they could not pay money they owed. Conditions in those prisons were horrible.

Oglethorpe meets with Yamacraw Indians, members of a Creek tribe

Oglethorpe worked on a committee dedicated to changing those prisons. He was especially outraged when he met a man whose wife had died while in prison with him. The man pleaded with the guards to bury his wife. They refused. The man died as he told his story to Oglethorpe. Oglethorpe and his committee knew that kind of punishment did not fit the crime.

At the same time, Britain was looking to start a colony as a buffer between the Spanish in Florida and the colony of South Carolina. Oglethorpe saw a chance to deal with two problems at once. He suggested that the colony be started by people who would otherwise be in debtor's prison. The British agreed.

But Oglethorpe knew the Native Americans would not just hand over their land. He needed to make a deal with the Creeks. He needed to win their trust.

By this time, Coosaponakeesa had changed her name to Mary. She also married John Musgrove, the wealthy son of a South Carolina leader. They started a trader's post in Creek territory at the request of the British. Both the British and the Creeks trusted Mary.

That made Mary the perfect choice when Oglethorpe needed an interpreter. He would be talking with the Yamacraw Indian leader, a 90-year-old *mico*, or chief, named Tomochichi. The Creeks were suspicious. They thought about going to war with the colonists. But Mary believed in the British. She convinced the Creeks that they would prosper by working with the colonists. Because of Mary, Oglethorpe was allowed to start the colony of Georgia.

Mary was more than an interpreter. She also argued Oglethorpe's position. She acted as a mediator, someone who helps create a bridge of trust between two different sides. The British trusted her so much that they asked her to start another trading post to the south. They wanted Mary to keep an eye on the Spanish from the new trading post.

The Creeks trusted her, too. She was of royal Creek blood, after all. Her people trusted her so much that they gave her thousands of acres of land.

But the British, for all their trust, refused to accept Mary's claim on the land. She argued with them about the land for

Mary Musgrove negotiating beside her husband in Savannah, Georgia

most of the rest of her life. They finally reached a compromise just a few years before her death. The British gave Mary and her husband a large amount of money and an island in return for "her service to the Crown."

Oglethorpe always knew Mary's value to the British. He was so grateful that he even gave Mary a diamond ring off his finger in 1742. He knew Mary had stopped a possible war with the Creeks. He knew that without Mary, the Georgia colony might not have survived.

Jonathan Edwards: Master Preacher

Reverend Jonathan Edwards believed in a strict reading of the Bible. He believed in dedicating everything to God. He was like the Puritans who started the American colonies in the 1600s.

But America in the 1700s moved away from that view. Edwards fought to bring it back.

Edwards was born in 1703 in East Windsor, Connecticut. He was a brilliant child. He spent a lot of time studying nature. He even wrote a paper about flying spiders that impressed experts 160 years later. But his true calling was the church.

Edwards went to Yale College at the age of thirteen. He planned to become a preacher like his father and his grandfather. He earned his Masters Degree in 1722. He then spent eight months at a small church in New York.

But he left after eight months. The church was too small to pay his salary. His father begged him to tutor at Yale. Edwards did not care for the idea. But he did it anyway.

Edwards was miserable. He wanted to be among the people. He wanted to preach. So in 1726, he became the associate pastor at his grandfather's church in Northampton, Massachusetts. He became the full pastor when his grandfather died in 1729.

Edwards spent 13 hours a day in his study. He spent hours on his knees, praying. He worked endlessly on his sermons. He was determined to be the most holy man he could be. And he wanted to spread God's word as widely as possible.

Jonathan Edwards

But religious dedication was slipping in the colonies —
until 1734. That is when a revival broke out in Northampton.
There was a sudden upswing in spirit in Edwards' church.
Religion was suddenly the only topic in town.

That was the beginning of "The Great Awakening," a period of renewed interest in religion. The movement swept across the colonies. It continued into 1741. Edwards became a strong and well-known figure during this period. In 1738, he wrote about the change in his own church in "A Faithful Narrative of the Surprising Work of God." He published several long sermons that are still studied by preachers today. And his revival sermons drew thousands of people.

Edwards was not an exciting speaker. He read from notes. His voice was even and calm. But what he said impressed people. His sermons were full of passion, even if they weren't delivered that way.

But his approach to church membership got him in trouble at home. He believed that church members should only be people who had been through conversion. That was said to happen when people were "saved" by God. Edwards believed that it did not matter what people did in their lives. God decided who would be converted.

Edwards also believed that those who had not experienced conversion should not be allowed to take communion, which was one of the important rituals of the church. But his church did not feel the same way. Edwards was voted out as pastor by his church in 1750.

Edwards then became a pastor in Stockbridge, Massachusetts for six years. He also became a missionary to 150 Mohican and Mohawk families in that region. And he found more time to write. He wrote four major works that dealt with issues such as free will and original sin.

Edwards became president of the College of New Jersey in 1758. (That school later became Princeton University.) He planned to do more writing. But he caught the smallpox disease. He died on March 22, 1758.

Edwards' legacy has lived on. He is considered one of the most important religious figures of American history. Once considered too old-fashioned for his own day, his words have stood the test of time. Many writers now point to Edwards as a modern figure. His writings still have the power to help Americans understand what is right and wrong in a stressful and confusing age.